BICYCLE LOTUS

SARA BACKER

Bicycle Lotus
Copyright © 2015 Sara Backer

Winner, 2015 Turtle Island Poetry Award

Turtle Island Quarterly sponsors the annual Turtle Island Poetry Award. Awards are chosen by the editors. More information available at http://fourdirectionpoetry.wix.com/turtleisland

Acknowledgments

I'm happy to have an opportunity to thank the editors of the following journals in which these pieces previously appeared, some in earlier versions:

The Avalon Literary Review: "Bicycle Lotus"
Cobra Lily: "Weeder Geese" (reprint)
Faultline: "Your Egret"
Montucky Review: "Inmates"
Poetry Northwest: "The Drowning Man"
Renovation Journal: "The Eye of the Beholder"
San Pedro River Review: "Ghost Owl"
Turtle Island Quarterly: "On Looking Like the Indian I'm Not," "A Predator's Dilemma," "Redwood Vision," "The Retreat," "That Darn Coyote Again," "This Is Just to Add," "Wasp Nest," "Weeder Geese," and "What Crows Don't Know"

I am profoundly grateful for the insightful original cover art by Katherine West.

To my lifelong poet friends whose comments inevitably improve and enrich my writing, Eric Paul Shaffer and Michael Spring: thank you always for what you inspire, encourage, and understand.

In memory of the sculptor Bill King (1924-2015), who raised my spirits over the years by telling me my poems were "the real deal."

First Left Fork Edition, December 2015
ISBN-13 978-0-692-58371-5

CONTENTS

Introduction, by Jared Smith	iv
Your Egret	3
Water Horse	4
The Beholder of the Eye	5
The Eye of the Beholder	6
Wasp Nest	7
A Predator's Dilemma	8
This Is Just to Add	11
Mica	12
Bicycle Lotus	13
On Looking Like the Indian I'm Not	14
Redwood Vision	18
That Darn Coyote Again	19
The Wolf Within	20
Weeder Geese	21
How Strong the Bond?	22
Citizen Coma	23
The Drowning Man	24
Ghost Owl	25
Inmates	26
The Retreat	27
My Focus Fails in Dhyana	28
What Crows Don't Know	29

INTRODUCTION

by
Jared Smith

There are a great many voices in this compact and fulfilling chapbook. There are men and women; predators and prey; coyote tricksters, frogs, skunks, geese, a water horse, "your own egret," and more. "So many boats and people!" as Sara Backer writes. And they all come together in one sweeping, complex and yet startlingly simple vision of unity. Even the frozen and lifeless elements that make up the bedrock of our planet and the fiery orbs that light our nights are a part of it. And Sara Backer does not separate herself from this unity, but sees herself in both dark moments and light as being of that unity.

This is an extraordinary collection of poems by an extraordinary poet.

The opening poem presents an exceptionally astonishing and lasting metaphor for the collection. *Your Egret*, the powerful, pure egret that asks entrance to the poet's opening world is seen up-close as being built of wires and dirty feathers and lice. Initially a flame of white purity, it fills its mouth and throat with frogs, slurping and bulging, filling itself with life-giving protein from the mud between its legs—and the reader is allowed to experience it all, nature's voice, like it or not in its indifferent give and take. It is there for the experiencing in its rawness, and only when the poet calls to it and tries to bring it close in order to own it, does its majesty vanish. Even in this opening poem, one finds that to understand the majesty of the wild you must experience it from both within yourself and outside of yourself—from the unity.

This powerful theme continues, while picking up additional narratives and layers of understanding. The mythical *Water Horse* appears in her next poem, up to its knees in the water we swim in, a part of our lives. In *The Beholder of the Eye* an assumed black dog, defined only by its description but certainly a creature of consciousness, observes and walks on a puddle of the water that a horse might be drinking from and grows wary as that puddle freezes over and crystallizes into a solid sheet of ice and detritus that the poet struggles to capture in words on her computer, and describes as an eye—looking perhaps from what is larger and deadlier and more filled with life than anything we can understand?

And here two poems later, in *Wasp Nest*, the poet pulls herself back for the first time from the wild by throwing poison created by mankind into a wasp nest so that "I won't fear the sting." This becomes a narrative of perception rather than conscious thought, and the first theme nears completion as Sara Backer breaks with her opening stylistic choice of lyric, visually rich poems to a thoughtful prose discussion over the quandary she is faced with by seeing all things—herself included—as one, and yet her need to assert herself as separate and as a predator among prey. "It's easy," she meditates, "to champion harmless herbivores like porcupines and deer, but protecting predators—especially ones that attack you—requires more commitment." And further "...I was a predator, too, with a need to defend myself and my nest. I chose to kill the queen."

This is not just a shifting of style or poetic craft, it is a shifting of speed and focus. It is the mark of a real master of her craft, demonstrating how to jar the reader's sensibility in order to renew experience and understanding. One is reminded here stylistically of the technique used in haiku and haibun—where each poem contains both vivid imagistic nonlinear thought in strict poetic meter and then a paragraph of meditation on those images and the thoughts that might but don't quite contain them, but the Japanese requirement of syllable count in the poems is of course here Americanized. And of course this is use of that technique for a whole segment of the collection, rather than within an individual poem, especially as it is used again. (This speaks eloquently for the collection itself being a poem in terms of vision, rather than a collection of poems, but I won't dwell on that.)

At this point alone, we have a very solid and stimulating collection of work, but there are many more discoveries to experience—many more layers and voices that come from within our interior and exterior lives. "The job is to make/us notice what is around us/ yet does not revolve around us. // This job is never done" she writes in *This is Just to Add*. What is perceived and seen may be or it may not be: the experience alone determines it, as she finds in discourse with the trickster Coyote. "*(Dude, get your tail out of my face!)*" Her vision is keen, and she struggles to fulfill her understandings with it, but "above the fog where I might see the ocean // were my vision not scorched/by the giant needle-splintered sun"—that hard disc of sun reflecting back the eye frozen on the forest floor. In accounting for the Trickster, one has to realize that all visions are equal in validity dependent on their view and point of view. "The truth of human experience is not one poem or the other, but both." A new layer of understanding takes form...and the collection goes onward.

In *The Wolf Within*, the poet tastes the wilderness and savagery within herself and recognizes its essentiality:

> We've fought fifty years,
> building invisible substance,
> bleeding and scarring.
> The wolfless don't understand
> my one-handed battle to live.
> No amount of kindness
> changes me.

And with that we move back into a domestic world, but one shaped with a recognition of the wilderness and savagery within us. "*Don't feel any moral qualms! We enjoy eating ourselves!*" Share in predation then, but do not exploit it. The poet now has a strong and yet slashing moral awareness—*not qualms but an awareness*—of social conditions within the domestic realm as well as within the wild since both are awake within her. She writes within the next poems scathing commentary on the Citizen Coma she finds our society in…of the death that comes over our citizenry when it loses awareness, and of how only that awareness can save us from the empty passageways that lie between "catheter and saline drip." We must not just name the animals and their places of habitat, she says, but know them. The wildness must take us by the scruff of the neck and bring us back, bring us to life, because nothing else will.

Okay, that's the gist of it, but I have never seen so much insight, understanding, passion, and fight packed into any chapbook before. This is what a chapbook should be all about—a precise and mind expanding voyage into a state of mind that could not be entered into through a longer work—and yet contains more than any work of similar size possibly could. Perhaps it is like the world it speaks of in that regard.

BICYCLE
LOTUS

Your Egret

The white bird stands
at your door. "I'm your egret."
Book in one hand,
drink in the other, you didn't
order an egret.

The egret shifts feet.
Snowball on wires.
Purity from a distance.
Up close, dirty feathers and lice.

You shut the door
and read and drink
all afternoon.

In your back yard, the egret
eats frogs:
plunge, snatch
—legs dangle from beak—
slurp, bulge.

You watch, afraid
it will clap its wings
and chase you away.

The egret walks slowly.
"Don't go!" you call out. "You're
my egret!"

The white bird stops.
Vanishes.

Water Horse

At a small dirt beach circled by pines,
Mr. Swanson taught us how to float and kick,
and then to crawl. We practiced breast and back strokes
between the buoys where our feet touched mucky bottom.

Our skill test was to swim to the island
across the narrowest part of lake.
My mother urged me not to try, as I was weak from illness,
but by August, Mr. Swanson thought I was ready.

I swam beside his boat as half a mile expanded
into my life: confusion, fatigue,
switching strokes, and treading water
clogged with white and yellow lilies.

Somehow, I made it. As I trembled with triumph
in a big blue towel, Mr. Swanson swapped oars
for the motor and steered our celebration ride
into the large part of lake we couldn't see from camp.

So many
boats and people!
And a horse up to her knees in water,
drinking.

The Beholder of the Eye

Loretta plunges into this puddle up to her shoulders,
black tail waving, lapping water. When she hauls herself out,
mud drips from her long white fur.

But a cold snap turned the puddle from black to white.
Loretta's paws slip on the sturdy surface.
The outer edges froze first, slowly squeezing concentric rings,

pushing the puddle into the semblance of an eye
with a giant iris and pupil in the middle, pine needles and oak leaves
trapped in the ice—painful splinters that can't be pulled out.

The woman, bundled in parka and scarves, aims the camera
she calls her "seeing-eye camera" as her own eyes, inflamed
and filmy, can no longer be believed.

At home, on her computer, she'll see what she saw.
The sadness of the flat white eye embedded in the lonely woods
pulls from her eyes small tears that freeze in her lashes.

She wonders if any water is left in the puddle,
in the deep center, below detritus and decay, even one drop.
With shepherd instinct, Loretta grows uneasy,

and noses the woman's hand. Time to go—the air
well below freezing and dangerous—yet the woman can't stop
watching the eye of ice, staring blindly beyond her.

The Eye of the Beholder

A bug
dive
bombs
smack
into
your
eye.

Man, you can't not
notice that.

Wasp Nest

Pernicious scritching:
yellow jacket jaws
building a spittle-paper nest.

The nest is egg-shaped:
elegant, functional. Far superior
to my sprawling, ugly house.

In the evening, I spray poison,
destroying art
so I won't fear the sting.

A Predator's Dilemma

To talk about wasps, I need to start with bees. As a child, I loved bees. In summer, I ran around outside in nothing but a homemade cotton sundress and flip-flops. We had an English border garden edged with a long swath of sedum that grew to ankle height, and honey bees would thrum in the low pink blossoms. I could see more amber-colored bees than flowers. My mother told me they wouldn't hurt me if I didn't bother them. When, wildly riding my tricycle or jumping rope, one would sting me, I believed it was a mistake and felt sorry for the death of the bee. The stings carried a sharp but fleeting pain, and I knew how to pull out the stingers and cover the bite with a stiff paste made of baking soda and water. By mid-summer, between bee, mosquito, ant, and spider bites, my legs were mostly pink bumps and white powder patches. My favorite bees were the big, solitary bumblebees that flew slowly and droned at a lower pitch. I taught myself to catch them and, barely touching them, gently stroked the soft fuzz on their backs. They often stayed in the cupped palm of my hand even though they could freely fly away.

Compared to bees, wasps seemed disproportionately large and thin. Wasps flew higher, in more erratic yet purposeful patterns; they lived in adult space and were not my concern. My first meeting with a wasp was at my grandmother's house. I leaned against the back of the garage at dusk, vaguely hoping to see a bluebird emerge from one of the wooden birdhouses my grandfather built and stuck on poles in his large vegetable garden. As I stood in that supreme state of doing nothing but observing, a yellow jacket flew directly toward me and stung me just to the left of my breast bone, precisely over my heart. The pain I experienced was not the ephemeral surprise of a honeybee sting, but a stabbing burning sensation that wouldn't quit. My skin swelled into a bump and I developed a slight fever. I did not go anaphylactic, but I recall someone saying I might be allergic to wasp venom. Along with feeling woozy and nauseous, I felt indignation, for I had done nothing to harm or alarm the wasp. That wasp taught me nature was not all live and let live.

So, at age seven, I began to grapple with the initial challenges of being an environmentalist. It's easy to champion harmless herbivores like porcupines and deer, but protecting predators—especially ones that attack you—requires more commitment.

Take, for example, the fisher, a tree-dwelling weasel slightly larger than a house cat with rounded ears and sleek fur. Seldom seen, the powerful and speedy fisher is capable of attacking prey with a bite at the base of the brain so quickly its prey may not know what happened. Fishers originally got a bad rap from farmers because one fisher will kill every chicken in the coop. Farmers who found dead chickens and fisher tracks the next morning assumed the fisher killed for sport which made it a "bad" animal—you know, like humans. What they didn't know is that fishers, unlike most predators, also eat carrion and will return to their kill sites to finish up what they left. Fishers need tons of protein daily to maintain their impressive muscles and glorious coats. Rumors about the viciousness of fishers continue because they will occasionally attack pet cats. Although studies of fisher stomachs and feces show that house cats are a mere garnish in their diet (they mostly eat squirrels), people assume their beloved pets are being eaten by fishers instead of the far more likely predator of the woods, coyotes, due to their false reputation. A few folks around here, spotting a glimpse of a fisher at dawn or dusk, will respond by loading their shotguns. Without fishers, the rodent population would burgeon. Beyond their practical purpose in the food chain, however, is their astonishing beauty. I wonder if some of the fisher-haters watched a fisher run if they would be less adamant about extinguishing them.

Wasps are beautiful, too. When I heard the delicate rustle of a wasp chewing, I was sitting on my door stoop. I looked around to find the nest. Not until I tipped my head back did I see pale gray hexagonal paper cells on the outdoor light directly over the front door. I hoped it might be a shy brown paper wasp, but its precise yellow markings made it a yellow jacket—who was way too close for comfort. Nine species of yellow jackets inhabit New Hampshire and all are aggressive.

Flashback to 1992 in Japan. All American wasps seem benign compared to the gigantic hornets of Asia. A *Vespa Mandarina Japonica* built a nest beside the door of my second floor apartment. This two-inch hornet zagged toward me every time I went in or out. I imagined a rerun of that stressful summer, constantly draping a large scarf over my head and hoping that was enough to confuse the hornet as I hurried through the danger zone between my door and my bicycle chained up downstairs.

I also thought about the children I tutored in my home (and possible allergies to wasp venom), along with visitors, the mail carrier, and my cat who liked to roll on the cement stoop. I had good reasons to destroy the nest-in-progress while only one queen was working solo and the nest was smaller than a golf ball. After the first larvae hatch, they help the queen enlarge the nest which can grow to house four or five thousand wasps.

On the other hand, wasps eat caterpillars, flies, and other soft-bodied insects, and happen to be the favorite cuisine of my favorite bird, common Eastern Phoebes, who nest outside my bedroom window year after year. (I once delayed house painting until the phoebe chicks fledged.)

Was it my moral obligation to set aside my own safety for the sake of wasps and phoebes and the food chain in general? I thought about the Jains, who lay on mattresses infested with bed bugs or fleas in order to feed them. The most devout Jain regarded it a duty to extinguish his own life for the cause of preserving other lives. But I was a predator, too, with a need to defend myself and my nest.

I chose to kill the queen as efficiently as possible.

This Is Just to Add

He asked: "Why do poets always
write about the minutiae of nature?"
I said: "Because that's the job." Of course,
poets also write about war, love, death, sex, gods—
that is to say, clocks, fudge, polyester,
defibrillators, and spray paint.
But the job is to make
us notice what is around us
yet does not revolve around us.

This job is never done,
and that's why I must tell you
about the young weasel I watched at sunrise,
perched in my plum tree like a sleek black cat,
who shook dry, mealy plums to the weedy ground
and sprang from the branch to eat.

Mica

Everything I respect begins
with porcupine and skunk.
I must defend myself.

Everything I value begins
with a brook:
buoyancy and rhythm.

Every piece of sky I breathe
has been touched by wings
of wasps and phoebes.

I'm learning how to breathe.
I hold my breath like sunshine
locked in ice.

Everything I think begins
with granite and mica.
I peel silver layers.

Bicycle Lotus

July in Japan—so many final exams!
Sunday, I ride a red bicycle
scavenged on Big Trash day.

After yesterday's typhoon,
the air is dry enough to breathe,
and I pedal beyond the university,
beyond Mitsubishi pencils
and Tamiya plastic models,
beyond the rice paddies
in shadeless heat.
Sweat hangs in my eye lashes.
I am too lonely to care that I'm lost,
mesmerized by the infinite spin
of spoke shadows on pale concrete.

I turn to escape the sun, and there,
in a ditch, is a perfect pink lotus.
Even without touching the petals,
without a sip of tea
pounded from its roots,
its healing power
releases me from my trance.
I photograph it, and remember
where I live.

On Looking Like the Indian I'm Not

The question is never "are you Indian?" but "which tribe are you?" The question distresses me. Only Indians ask me this—(I use the term "Indian" because my friends call themselves that, not to perpetuate disrespectful Colonialism)—an assumption ventured during bond-building, and I don't want to make a new friend feel wrong. Nor do I want to be the insufferable white woman who claims an "Indian Princess" as an ancestor or crushes on Native American culture in a self-involved quest for instant spirituality. I quickly plead guilty to my Caucasian forebears, which is the truth—but not the whole story.

European descendants perceive me as one of them due to my fair skin, curly hair, and tiny nose. What American descendants notice is my dark eyes and wide cheekbones that shape my face into a hexagon. I have a big face. I also have a big mouth, which I sometimes blame on Coyote, as in: "I'm sorry—Coyote made me say that." Which most white people don't do, and perhaps I shouldn't.

#

The mythological Coyote is a trickster with a wicked sense of humor associated mostly with tribes west of the Mississippi River. He is a spiritual cousin of the Scandinavian Loki, European Reynard-the-Fox and Japanese fox-like *kitsune*. Coyote is sometimes a god or half-god, sometimes human, and sometimes shares features with the animal coyote, *Canis latrans*. Several stories have him introducing death to the world or creating humans. He causes big trouble fooling others. He tortures and is tortured. Sometimes he marries and other times he's a perennial player. He can be cast as a main character or walk-on, tends to be more annoying than charming, and can be refreshingly pointless. Despite or because of his intrusion into everyone's business, his big ego, and his carefree manner, Coyote is very human. It's easy to get mad at Coyote, but hard to stay mad. For example, he jumped into my essay and claimed this entire paragraph. While this was not my plan, I haven't cut the paragraph—yet. (*Dude, get your tale out of my face!*)

#

I do not believe I have Indian ancestors lurking in the question marks in my family tree between Adriaen Backer's nameless third son who sailed from Amsterdam to New Netherlands in 1640 and Casper Backer born in 1752. The Backers settled near Newark, New Jersey, home of the Wolf sector of the Lenni-Lenape tribe whom Dutch settlers called Delaware Indians. The Turtle and Turkey sectors inhabited central and southern New Jersey and eastern Pennsylvania. The "len" of Lenape means "people" and the prefix "Lenni" reinforces that: they are the people of the people, as in original or genuine people. Other Algonquin Nation tribes referred to the Lenape as the grandfather tribe, and the Lenape's Great Turtle myth may have been the origin of the term Turtle Island (it was either the Lenape or Iroquois). The influx of Dutch settlers brought battles and smallpox; the Lenni-Lenape population dwindled by about 90% between the arrival of Henry Hudson in 1609 to the birth of my great-great-great-great-grandfather Casper. I hope the pre-Revolution Backers lived peaceably with the Wolves, but it's more likely my ancestors killed Lenni-Lenape than married them. I'll never know.

What matters to me is that four or five generations of question marks whose gene pool eventually created me lived in the same place and time as the Lenape tribe. They survived the same snowy winters and muggy summers, ate the same corn, squash, and beans, hunted the same deer and rabbits, farmed the same sandy loam, watched the same sun rising from the Atlantic ocean and setting in the Ramapo Mountains. The Lenape believed (as I do) that they learned how to live from what lived around them, much as immigrants learned from native tribes. For this, I owe the Lenni-Lenape not only my respect but my existence. In that sense, I belong to that tribe: not that I am one of them, but that they own me, a child of Caucasians who were born for generations on land that was inhabited by (and should rightfully still "belong" to) the original people. Thus, I owe and am owned.

#

How do I observe this debt?

I read that the woodchuck was a one of the Lenape's sacred animals and vowed never to harm one. In other places, I read the muskrat was the actual sacred animal. Fine: I won't harm either one. Same goes for turkeys, turtles, and wolves.

I once watched a turhen eat all the beet seedlings in my garden. She was methodical about it, snapping off the nascent leaves at the ground with her curved beak, going down the row as orderly as I'd planted them. A woodchuck ate most of my cucumber patch, one of the few vegetables I can grow in my sandy soil. While gardeners in my neighborhood are dismayed that I don't shoot, poison, or trap them, I am dismayed by their eagerness to kill the native wildlife. Animals live in a world of right now. If I wanted to eat beet seedlings or cucumber plants at the same time they did, both turkey and woodchuck would have yielded to me. How could I kill an animal for the crime of not understanding my intention of saving food for later? The land was their habitat long before it was mine; they deserve to eat what is in their territory. Besides, unlike them, I always have the option of purchasing vegetables at the local farm stand.

In addition to co-existence, I practice the usual eco-lifestyle—recycling, minimizing use of chemicals, reducing waste, etc. I am an ardent enemy of lawns which require ungodly amounts of pollution to maintain. My front yard is covered with wild violets (which deer eat) and scrubby blueberries (which rodents and birds eat). I don't do this to change the world. I am well aware that anything we do on a personal level is minuscule compared to the ongoing pillage of nature by corporations, but in my small way I attempt to acknowledge a large debt to the land. I call the woodchuck by its Lenape name: *munhake*.

#

The Lenapes didn't have Coyote in their mythology, but they did have a trickster figure called "Crazy Jack" or "Little Jack" known as Wehixamukes, Kupahweese, Cheekiitha, or Chekitha. In these stories, Wehixamukes follows directions to the letter, not the meaning. For example, when he accidentally cuts his hand with an axe, a hunter tells him to tie bark to the wound to heal it. He climbs a tree and ties himself into it. When the hunter finds him and tells him he should have cut the bark from the tree, instead, Wehixamukes replies: "I'd have done that if you had told me!" I love the way he demands exactitude in wording. He is a teacher of poets.

#

Last, I want to say that people often see what they look for more than what they look at. When I visited France, French people thought I was French—until I spoke. When I visited Panama, Panamanians thought I was Costa Rican because of how I spoke, as I'd learned Spanish living in Costa Rica. In Japan, Japanese friends asked if I had Japanese ancestry. And when an ex-boyfriend (Navajo) complained about how "white" an acquaintance was until I got irritated and pointed out, hey, I'm white, too, he replied: "You're not nearly as white as he is." So, perhaps I am a racial Rorschach. Wherever I wander, I try to learn from the life that surrounds me and maybe that attitude (along with brown eyes) triggers the question.

Thus ends my white woman ethnicity narrative.

#

Fake out! I'm back with an addendum. (*Dude—an addendum?*)

Sometimes, my close observation of nature leads me to write a poem that others might misinterpret as sentimental (the horror!). Often, that poem will call to Coyote to express the banal side. Here's an example:

Redwood Vision

"The redwoods, once seen, leave a mark or create a vision that stays with you always." —*John Steinbeck*

My first redwood forest planted a vision
of a house connecting earth to sky.

A bedroom in the basement roots, pitch dark for sleep,
where dreams feed on thick river silt.

A kitchen in the lower trunk, eye level with black bears
foraging salmonberries in misty understory.

Azaleas make their own pink light
in deeply dappled shade.

Higher up, I sit on a slanted porch, ear level
with wingbeats of hovering flycatchers.

Closets are crevices in rough, grainy bark
holding scrolls of poems and maps.

I climb a stairway of erratic burls up to a crow's nest
above the fog where I might see the ocean

were my vision not scorched
by the giant needle-splintered sun.

A few days after drafting "Redwood Vision," Coyote showed up and dictated this poem:

That Darn Coyote Again

I tell him when I said redwood, I meant the tree,
one word, not two—
—yeah, sure, he interrupts, the tree.
Women always want to see the tree.

No use talking to him about habitat
while he's pissing on azaleas.
I have second thoughts about this camping spot.
Not thrilled about smelling his urine.

I came alone to be alone. He was lounging around
the park station. Him with his creepy-charming smile,
rotten teeth, and long-winding jokes. Followed me
like a—I know who you are!

Coyote says he never heard of no coyote,
but if I want to brag to my white folk
that I fucked a full-blooded Tolowa…
well, maybe he could help with that.

The truth of human experience is not one poem or the other, but both. This defies the nature of nature literature, as journals that would publish "Redwood Vision" tend not to care for "That Darn Coyote Again" and vice versa. And then there's the whole appropriation issue in your face, again: when white people write about Coyote, is it usurpation or acceptance?

The Wolf Within

No amount of kindness
or understanding changes
the wolf that eats me.
The wolf isn't hungry;
she attacks because she is wolf
and can do nothing less
or more.

I restrain her with a rope
made of mountain roots,
nerves of a brown bear,
spittle that binds a phoebe nest,
antibiotics and corticosteroids.
Even so, she clenches my hand
between her jaws.

We struggle, angry, neither
free of the other—an endless cycle
of relapse and recovery.
When I find a potion to weaken her,
she develops immunity.
I gain strength, too, fighting her
in isometric symmetry.

We've fought fifty years,
building invisible substance,
bleeding and scarring.
The wolfless don't understand
my one-handed battle to live.
No amount of kindness
changes me.

Weeder Geese

The small white geese are easy.
I need only raise my right hand
to make them swerve left,
or my left to make them move right.

The fields are fenced to keep the geese
eating Bermuda grass,
clover, and horsetail
between pungent spearmint rows.

Goslings work best, enjoying food
more than sex. A hungry goose
will dig nubs of grass, even eat the roots.
A fighting goose is a feast.

I remind myself they are meant to be used.
But as I stumble down my muddy path,
and pause to unfold a silver wrapper
off a sliver of gum, I sometimes see

wild geese flying a ragged victory V,
feel twinges of pain in my tired shoulders,
and sense a shadow in the sky
raising an arm behind me.

Because geese eat grass and young weeds as quickly as they appear but do not touch some cultivated crops (primarily cotton, corn, strawberries, and mint), farmers use them to weed their fields in place of expensive hand labor or hoeing machines. Unlike humans and machines, geese work well in wet weather and mud.

How Strong the Bond?

The bull on the bottle of glue delivers the same myth as the chicken with a checked napkin tied around its neck, holding a knife and fork with feathers (somehow), eager to dig into a plate of fried chicken. *Don't feel any moral qualms! We enjoy eating ourselves!*

There was a cow I felt affection for, a brown and white calf with a tender gaze. The only cow in a pen of sheep, his presence kept them safer from coyotes. He disappeared in December to become someone's roast beef. I miss him.

But the smirking bovine logo with that unruly cowlick between his horns has wise guy eyes that see through the charade. He's one tough bull—a Marlon Brando bull, defiant as if his hooves and bones and skin had not been boiled into a substance the color and viscosity of melted mozzarella, with that smell that puts everyone in elementary school.

This bull stands for the final sacrifice of an animal with no more milk or beef or leather for us to use, who now "bonds strong for all your needs" safely, without toxins. And this is a lie: for the glue this bull adorns is synthesized from petroleum with a balance of polymers and tackifiers to make a goo viscous and strong.

I might choose to believe he chortles in triumph—*ha-ha, gluemakers, I'm alive!* But I suspect his cartoon head is there to make us feel we are exploiters, too: guilty of eating his ribs and rump. Through the fallacy of equivalency, the lie of the logo keeps us complacent.

I might have to answer for killing half a dozen cows in my lifetime, but I do not impoverish a million people to make a billion dollars. I do not melt the ice cap to squeeze black blood out of the earth's veins. This glue will not bond me with the ruling class.

When the time comes, I'm prepared to boil my own bones.

Citizen Coma

I am prepared to bring all the water
of the world to your hospital bed,
from the oily boat-crunching teeth
of North Atlantic waves to the window
cleaning blue of Caribbean coves,
cappuccino flood waters of Sri Lanka,
foam-filled gutters of China, African
pea soup puddles, and beef broth
brewed by Brazilian mines. How long
can you survive between your saline drip
and catheter? If I throw a melting glacier
in your gray face, will you wake?
Will a cabernet blood bath revive you?
You lie, your eyes forever shut,
dreaming of kings and crowns.

The Drowning Man

When he jumped over the railing of the bridge,
I jumped after him. That fast, that simple. I had
to find him in stagnant darkness, break him loose,
haul him to the noisy surface (not easy with water-
weighted coats and shoes), sidestroke him to land,
pinch his nose, tip his chin and force my breath twice
into his numb lungs. Two fingers below his sternum,
jab my palm on his diaphragm fifteen times.

The rescue squad scolded me, of course. *Always
call 911 first—never go in alone—I could have died myself.*
Sensible advice for saving strangers, not husbands.
But tubed on the stretcher, foil blanket tucked around him,
pushed into the ambulance like a baked potato in the oven,
he looked like the stranger he had been all along.

Ghost Owl

I ran all the way to the river last night,
to return to the place you skipped
that flat stone with the white ring
seven times. We shook open folding chairs.
Rain splashed into our wine.
We could always count on rain.

I can't find the path we used to walk.
The pines have moved, green branches
gone brown. The sky is a ghost
from treetop to ground.
Was the barn owl we saw
a ghost owl, too?

Now, I'm the bad wife
to a good man who needs me.
I ran all the way to the river
where a river no longer ran.

Inmates

I hear there is a fat skunk, all white,
who waddles in the yard followed by two kits
the men call *babies*.
I hear about a pair of chipmunks and raccoons
that hang around the kitchen after chow.
A hummingbird appears some mornings,
a gray-tailed hawk at noon,
and at night, feeding on mosquitoes, bats carve
dark curves in the darkening sky.

In the windowless concrete room
where we unlock ideas from books,
I am impressed the men all know
each bird and animal the others describe.
They can pinpoint their locations
in the prison they inhabit.

The Retreat

The five of us were asked to bring
one small thing we couldn't live without.
We carried keys, photographs, a passport,
a wedding ring, and serious prescription medication
we thought we would honor in ceremony.
Instead, we were told
to throw them into the ravine.
It took as long as it took.

We stood
clutching,
thinking,
glancing
down.

I was first to toss twenty-two countries away,
but I was cheating. Unlike the others,
I could get another passport; this one
would get me out of here, now.

The man with the keys went next.
We hiked downhill together,
discussing the meaning of the word
retreat.

We reached his car in the lot: locked.
Looked at each other and laughed.
We had our feet.

My Focus Fails in Dhyana

Sitting on the ground, breathing—

I hear the sharp raspy song of a phoebe
returned to build a nest against my house: *fee bee, fee bee...*

Who was I before illness and injury?
Before I was warped by money and work?

Fee bee isn't accurate. A signature buzz distinguishes
phoebe from chickadee to the cadence of *know what? Fzz bzz?*

I glimpse erratic fanfare of gray and white wings
as this phoebe catches something mid-air...

Who was I before the overwhelming material
of existence? Before parents? Before language?

Gray tail twitches, bewitches. *Fzz bzz? Fzz bzz?*

I remember pine needles, blue sky, and cirrus clouds.
Me as a baby, wanting to be let loose into the woods.

Easily distracted outside alone in love with what I see and hear.

Know what? I'd rather watch this phoebe
weave into her new spring nest a silver strand of tinsel.

What Crows Don't Know

My visitors don't know I only pretend
to be unconscious because they bore me.
I hear phrases—*it's so sad—relatively young—
didn't have much—end of pain—perhaps it's best—*
and only when one says my name
do I understand they are talking about me!

The crows outside laugh with me; they know
I'll come around again. I have been ill
since I was six, one foot trailing in the gutter
of death for decades, yet keeping my balance,
resilient as a dandelion, adept at squeezing
my life into sidewalk cracks. Yet when I try to open
my eyes, to burst out of this bed (*ta-da!*), I can't.

Why is it so hard this time? I hear *limited life*
and *kept to herself* and wonder
why my thoughts don't move my lips.
I call a big favor from one who owes me,
whose life I have saved and defended.

Woodchuck!
Take me back!

And he does, the scruff of my neck in his teeth.
I return to the world where I can not
communicate with woodchucks.
The crows are gone. I'm tired; my body aches.

I suppose it will get harder each time, until I run dry
of favors in one world and friends in the other
who will finish me off with *sorry* and *sad*.
I will never have the last word about myself.

ABOUT THE AUTHOR

Sara Backer has climbed Mt. Fuji at night, swum among dolphins off the coast of Costa Rica, sung on street corners in Vienna, run for State Representative, and published a novel (*American Fuji*). She currently writes short fiction and poetry in the woods of New Hampshire, teaches at the University of Massachusetts at Lowell, and leads reading groups in a men's prison. Her writing has been honored with fellowships from the Djerassi Resident Artist Program and Norton Island Residency Program. Her work has appeared in numerous journals including *Poetry, Carve, Poetry Northwest, Seattle Review, Slant, Southern Poetry Review, Gargoyle, The Pedestal Magazine,* and *So to Speak* as well as international journals such as *Arc Poetry Magazine* (Canada), *The Rialto* (UK), *Allegro* (UK), *Hermes Poetry Journal* (UK), *New Welsh Reader* (UK), and *Crannóg* (Ireland). For more information, visit her web site: sarabacker.com.

www.ingramcontent.com/pod-product-compliance
Lightning Source LLC
Chambersburg PA
CBHW070047070426
42449CB00012BA/3178